NEW MODULAR SCIENCE
for GCSE

MODULE *Waves and Radiation*

Spread

Cover photograph *An ultrasound image of a foetus*

1 The radiation family

Meet the family

All living things need a constant supply of energy to live. The Sun radiates this energy to Earth so the energy is often referred to as **radiation**. Different types of radiation represent different amounts of energy. Like members of any family, the different types of radiation are given different names.

Members of the radiation family transfer different amounts of energy from the Sun to the objects in their path.

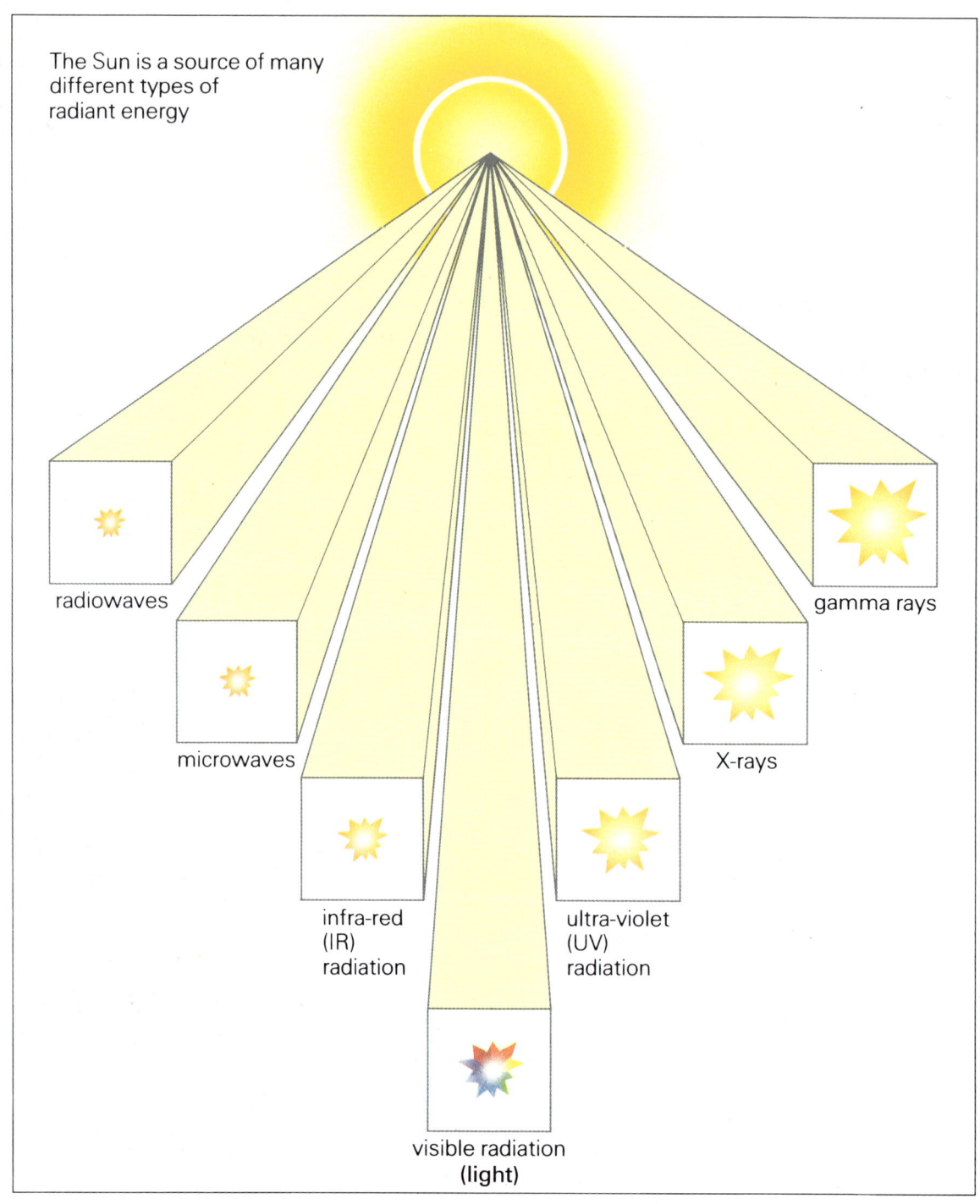

The Sun is a source of many different types of radiant energy

radiowaves

microwaves

infra-red (IR) radiation

visible radiation **(light)**

ultra-violet (UV) radiation

X-rays

gamma rays

Other things in common

Like members of any family, radiations from the Sun have other things in common besides being able to transfer energy. Much of what they have in common is related to how they travel or move.

They all move as waves.

▲ Waves of radiation have troughs and crests just like waves in the sea.

They all travel in space.

▲ Satellites in space catch beams of radiation that carry messages from one part of Earth and send them back to another.

All the types of radiation shown opposite are called **electromagnetic radiation**.

Read on to find out about other ways of producing these radiations besides the Sun. You will also discover how each member of the family is different, and how these differences lead to different ways of using them.

Water waves and radiation waves are not the only way of transferring energy waves. You will learn how energy is transferred as sound waves when you talk to someone else and by shock waves beneath the Earth's surface.

They all travel in straight lines.

▲ Beams of light are just one example of how radiations travel in straight lines.

They all travel at the same speed.

All radiation travels 186 000 metres every second – some of the radiation family may be used to speak to your family on the other side of the Earth!

2 Waves – what are they?

If you throw a stone into a pond, the stone creates a disturbance in the water. This disturbance is called a ripple or a small **wave**. The wave travels across the pond and, as it travels, it transfers energy. As a result, a leaf in the path of the wave would bob up and down. You may have created a similar type of wave by moving the end of a rope. As you have seen, there are many other types of waves such as light and all other forms of electromagnetic radiation.

A wave has to have a source of energy (for example, the Sun). Waves transfer energy from a source to other places without any matter being transferred.

A wave is a regular pattern of disturbance.

The size of waves

Any sailor will tell you that parts of some oceans in the world can be very dangerous because of the huge size of their waves. Huge waves can create great disturbances in the water. The maximum height or disturbance of a wave is called its **amplitude**. The larger the height or the amplitude of the wave, the more energy it transfers. Electromagnetic waves also have different amplitudes. Microwaves with large amplitudes can transfer more energy than those with small amplitudes. As a result they can cook food faster.

Waves with large amplitudes can transfer enough energy to capsize ships.

The length of waves

Suppose, as part of an exercise in measurement, one of your tasks was to find the length of the gap between your school railings. You wouldn't measure the gap between the top of one rail and the bottom of the other. Instead you'd measure the gap between two identical points on each railing. The measurement of wavelength uses the same idea. The wavelength is the distance in metres between a point on one wave and an identical point on the next wave. This **wavelength** is usually represented by the Greek letter lamda(λ).

The wavelength is the distance between two points with similar disturbance

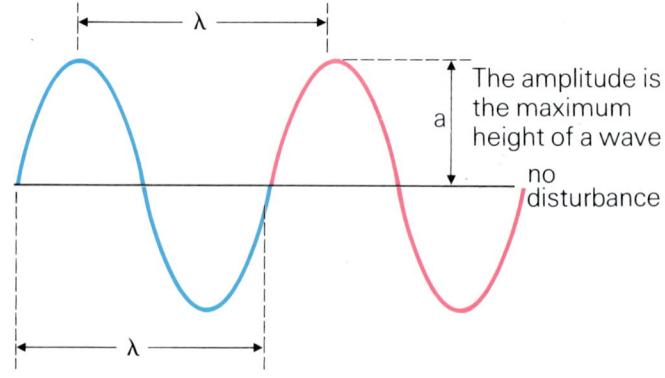

The amplitude is the maximum height of a wave

no disturbance

Two characteristics of a wave are its wavelength and amplitude.

The frequency of waves

If you sit on the edge of a swimming pool with your feet in the water and swing your legs you create a wave. The faster you move your feet through the water the more waves of the same size you produce. In other words the more energy you (as the source of the wave) produce, the more waves you need to transfer this energy. The waves are produced more frequently.

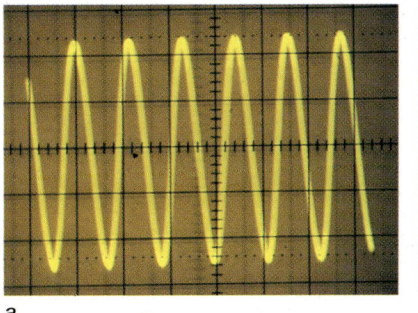
a

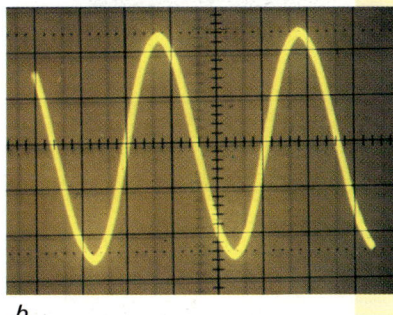
b

The shorter the wavelength, the greater the frequency of the wave.

The number of waves produced by a source in one second is called the **frequency** of the wave, and is measured in hertz (Hz). You may already be familiar with the frequency of some radio-waves such as BBC Radio 1 on 1089 kilohertz (a kilohertz or kHz is 1000 Hz). Look at the photos which show you two waves of different frequency. If the frequency of the first wave is 6 Hz, the frequency of the second wave is 2 Hz.

Types of waves

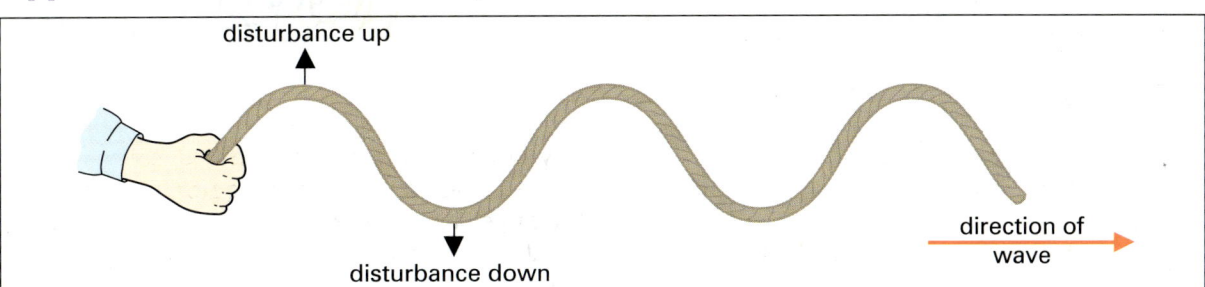

The disturbance of the rope is at right angles to the direction in which the wave travels.

A wave sent down a rope by moving one end shows you that the particles in the rope do not travel along the wave. They are, however, moved up and down, at right angles to the direction in which the wave travels. This type of wave is called a **transverse wave**. Water waves are also transverse waves. The troughs and crests of the wave move up and down at right angles to the direction in which the wave is travelling. Light waves are also transverse waves, but do not need a substance such as water to carry them – they can travel through space or a vacuum. You will meet another type of wave on page 11, which is about sound waves.

1 Name the two ways of creating a wave described in the first paragraph on the facing page.

2 A dimmer switch can be used to alter the brightness of a light bulb. What happens to the amplitude of the light waves as the light gets dimmer? Explain your answer.

3 Look at the wave diagram on the facing page. Suppose this is the number of waves produced by a source in one second.
  a What is the frequency of the wave?

  b Draw a wave with the same frequency but twice the amplitude.
  c Draw a wave with the same amplitude but half the frequency.

4 Gamma radiation transfers more energy than UV radiation. Which one would you expect to have the greater frequency? Explain your answer.

5 a What type of wave travels along ropes and across the surface of water?
  b How is the disturbance in such a wave related to the direction it is moving in?

3 Travelling waves

Seeing the light

You may have noticed that if you dive into a swimming pool the waves that you create travel across the surface of the water and bounce back or **reflect** off the side of the pool. Light waves behave in the same way.

You are able to see objects because light from them enters your eyes. Some objects, such as the Sun, give out their own light. But you see most objects because light bounces off their surface – the light is said to be **reflected**. Not all the light that hits an object is reflected. Some is taken in or absorbed by the object, usually as heat. This means less light enters your eyes so the object appears darker. The darker the surface of an object, the less the light is reflected and the more it is absorbed so the warmer it becomes.

You can see the magazine because some of the light from the lamp reflects off the magazine into your eyes.

Reflections

Rays of light often meet the surface of an object at an angle in much the same way that a snooker ball meets the cushion of the snooker table at an angle. Just like a snooker ball, the angle at which the ray leaves the surface is the same as the angle at which it meets the surface. Some surfaces are rough. If parallel rays of light hit rough surfaces they are reflected in *all* directions. This means that not all the light enters your eyes so the surfaces appear matt or unpolished. Other surfaces are very flat. Parallel rays of light that meet smooth, flat surfaces are reflected in only *one* direction. Most of the light enters your eyes so the surfaces appear shiny or polished.

A flat surface appears polished or shiny because most of the light is reflected into your eyes.

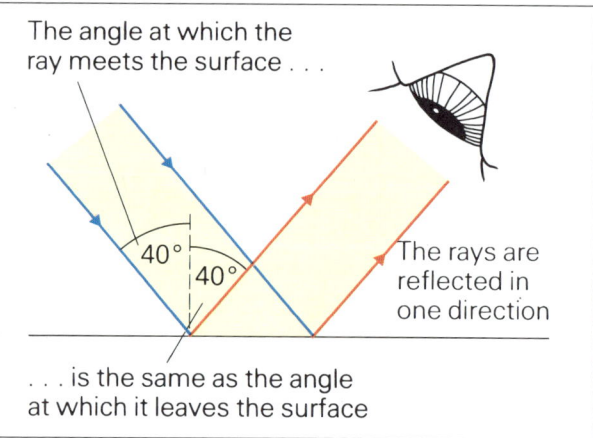

The angle at which the ray meets the surface . . .

40°
40°

The rays are reflected in one direction

. . . is the same as the angle at which it leaves the surface

Bending waves

Water waves can travel in straight lines across the surface of water. These straight waves can, however, be bent. This happens when they cross the boundary between deep and shallow water at an angle. If they meet the boundary head on – at right angles – they are not bent. This bending is caused by a change in the speed of the waves. The waves travel more slowly in the shallow water so the end of the wave that crosses the boundary first lags behind the other end. This bending of waves is called **refraction**.

Water waves are refracted when they pass from deep to shallow water.

Playing tricks

You may have noticed that when you use a straw with a drink the straw appears bent. This happens because you are looking at the straw in two different materials – the drink and air. Light behaves differently in the two different materials. It still travels in straight lines but it moves more slowly in the drink than in the air in the same way that water waves move more slowly in shallow water. This causes the light from the straw in the drink to change direction or bend when it meets the air. This bending of light is called **refraction**. The light tricks you into thinking the straw is bent because it has been refracted.

Refraction of light makes the straw look bent.

The speed of waves

Different types of waves move at different speeds. A wave moving across water moves very slowly compared to a light wave which can travel from London to New York in about 1/60th of a second. Concorde takes over two hours!

The speed of waves (v) is related to their frequency (f) and wavelength (λ) by the formula below:

$$v = f\lambda$$

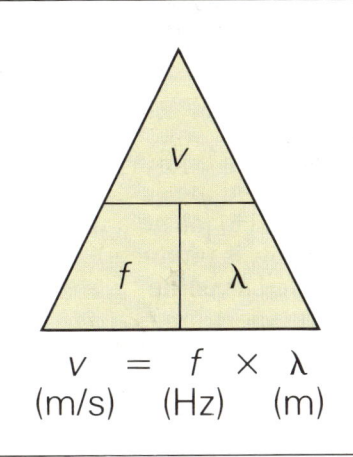

$$v = f \times \lambda$$
$$\text{(m/s)} \quad \text{(Hz)} \quad \text{(m)}$$

The formula can be put into a triangle to make calculations easier. If f is equal to v/λ, what is λ in terms of v and f?

1 Why do you think that the roof of a black car is hotter than the roof of a white car in summer?

2 Draw a diagram showing three parallel rays striking a rough surface. Show how the rays of light are reflected.

3 What is the difference in the behaviour of waves when they are reflected and refracted?

4 a What causes waves to refract?
   b Give two examples of refraction.
   c When would light not be refracted?

5 State two similarities in the behaviour of light beams and ripples moving across the surface of water.

6 Use the 'triangle' formula to help you to find the missing values below. Don't forget to include the units.

v(m/s)	f(Hz)	λ(m)
?	10	2
100	?	5
400	8	?

4 Bending light

Bending the beam

Refraction of light occurs when it travels from one transparent material to another, such as from air to glass. Refraction takes place at the boundary between the two materials. Imagine a dotted line drawn at right angles through the boundary where the ray of light meets it. The ray of light leaving the boundary bends away or towards this dotted line, or 'normal'. The direction of bending depends on the two materials on either side of the boundary. The diagram shows you what happens to a ray of pure yellow light passing through a glass prism. The ray of light bends towards the normal when going from air to glass.

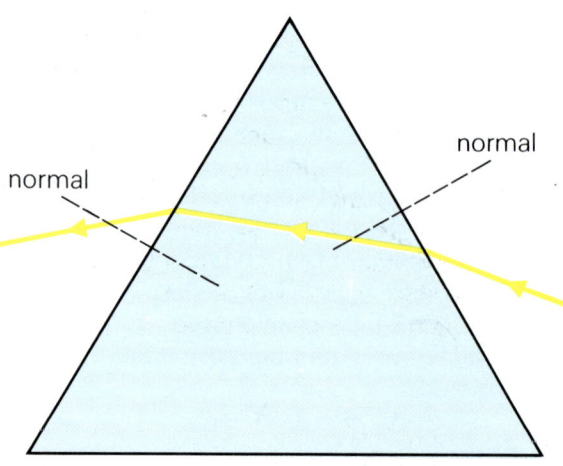

Light is refracted twice when it passes through a glass prism.

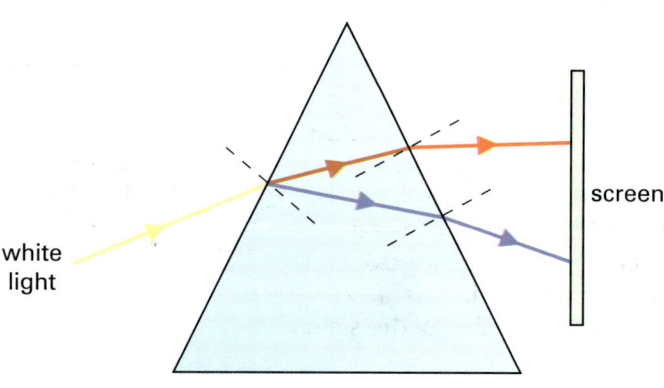

A prism separates white light into different colours.

A question of angles

Think about a ray of light which is being refracted as being in two parts. The ray of light before it is bent is called the **incident** ray. The ray of light after it has been bent is called the **refracted** ray. The amount that the refracted ray is bent depends on the incident ray. To be more exact, it depends on the *angle* between the incident ray and the normal. This is called the **angle of incidence**. The bigger this angle, the more the light is bent away from the normal – the more it is refracted. As well as being refracted, some of the light is also reflected from the boundary between the glass and the air.

Producing a Rainbow

If a ray of white light is passed through a prism and the light leaving is allowed to fall on a white screen, a rainbow is produced. This rainbow is called a **visible spectrum**. The spectrum is produced because white light is a mixture of different colours. These colours are bent or refracted by different amounts when they pass through the prism. Red light is refracted the least and violet light the most.

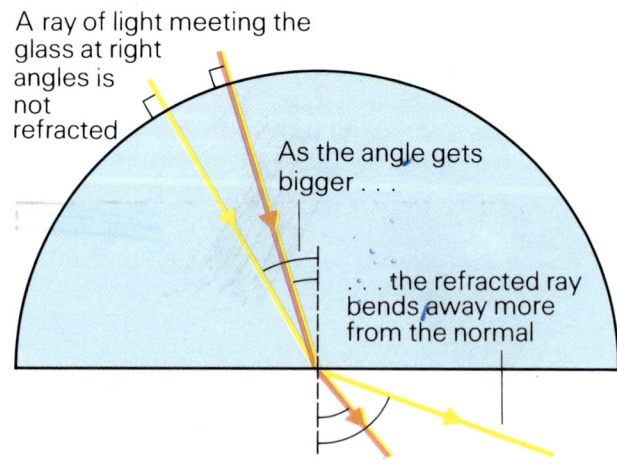

The amount the light is bent depends on the angle of incidence.

Now you see it . . . now you don't!

If you shine a light through a glass block common sense tells you that it should come out the other side. However, as you have already seen with the bent straw on page 7, light can do unexpected things. At a certain angle of incidence the refracted ray is bent so much that it travels along the edge of the glass instead of into the air. This angle is called the **critical angle**. Look at the diagram opposite. What is the critical angle from glass to air? If the angle becomes greater than the critical angle, the light is not refracted at all. It is reflected back into the glass block so that no light comes out the other side! This is called **total internal reflection**.

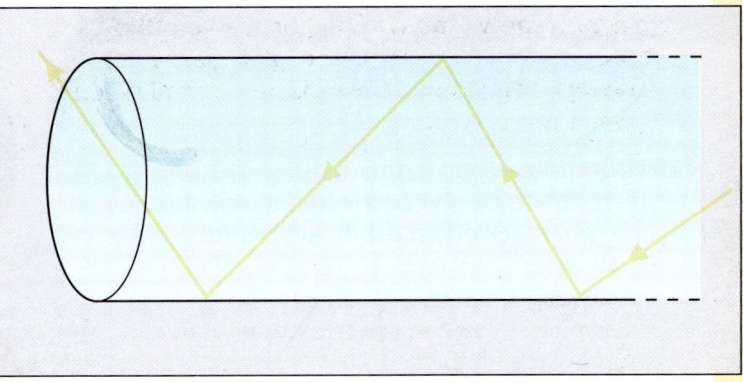

When the angle of incidence is 42°
air
42°
glass
. . . the ray travels along the boundary

When the angle of incidence is greater than 42°
air
glass
60° 60°
. . . the light is reflected

If the angle of incidence is greater than the critical angle, the light is reflected.

Seeing round corners

If you can make light reflect once inside a glass block then you can make it do so many times. Because of repeated total internal reflections, when light travels down a glass fibre, or **optical fibre**, all of it stays inside the fibre until it emerges from the other end. The flexibility of the fibre means it can be used by doctors to look inside a person's body. When used in this way, it is called an **endoscope**.

Light travelling along optical fibres is used not only to see in awkward places but also to carry information. An optical fibre, using light waves, can carry about 370,000 telephone conversations. Copper cables, using electrical signals, can carry only about 2000 conversations. The optical fibre is also lighter, smaller and easier to handle and there is less weakening of the signal.

Repeated internal reflections make the light travel along the optical fibre.

1 The diagram below shows two rays of light meeting a glass block. Copy the diagram and complete the path of the rays through the block.

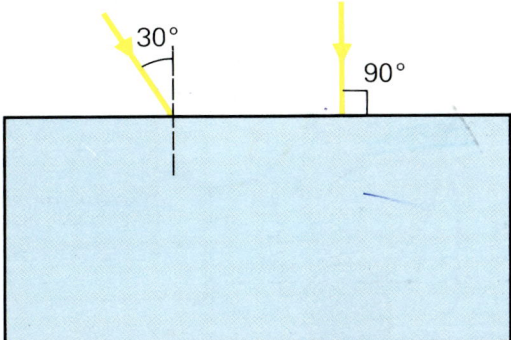

30°
90°

2 Green light is refracted more than red but less than violet. Draw a ray diagram showing white light being split up into red, green and violet light.

3 Copy the diagram below and complete the path of the ray of light through the prism.

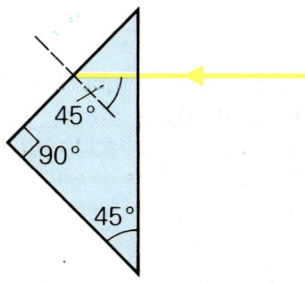

45°
90°
45°

4 State two uses of optical fibres.

5 What advantages do optical fibres have over copper cables for carrying information?

5 Sound and communication

Good vibrations

You live in a world of many different **sounds**. Whatever the sources of these sounds, they all have one thing in common. Like heat or light, sound is a form of **energy**. All sound is produced by materials moving to and fro, or *vibrating*. A cymbal vibrates if you hit it and this produces a sound. You can feel the vibrations if you touch the cymbal lightly. If you hold the cymbal firmly it stops vibrating and so produces no sound.

◀ *Sounds are produced when you make materials vibrate.*

Changing sound

You can't see sound waves but you can detect them using a microphone. This microphone can be connected to an instrument called an **oscilloscope**. An oscilloscope has a screen on it much like a television. When you speak into the microphone you can see a 'picture' of the sound wave on the screen.

Look at the 'pictures' on the screens. (You may find it helpful to refer to pages 4–5 about waves.)

The amplitude of the wave increases as the loudness of the voice increases.

The frequency of the wave increases as the pitch of the voice becomes higher.

A person with a soft high-pitched voice produces small waves which are close together (they have a high frequency)

A person with a loud high-pitched voice produces large waves which are close together

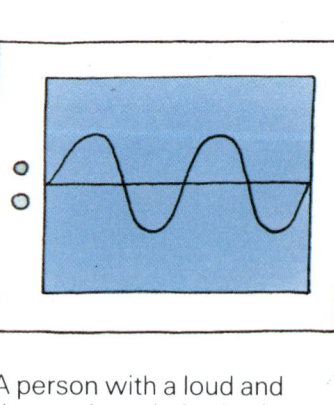

A person with a loud and deep or low pitched voice produces larger waves which are far apart (they have a low frequency)

Sound travelling ...

Whether speaking to your friends or listening to your favourite music, you are aware that sound travels from one place to another. However, sound needs a material to 'carry' it.

Air is quite good at carrying sound. If you have ever used a bicycle pump, you will have experienced the sensation of air being springy. A vibrating object passes on its sound vibrations to the air. The air behaves like a spring and becomes squashed in some parts and stretched in others. This movement through a material such as air is called a **sound wave**. The disturbance in the wave is along the same direction as that in which the wave travels. This means that the material gets squashed and stretched. This type of wave is called a **longitudinal wave**.

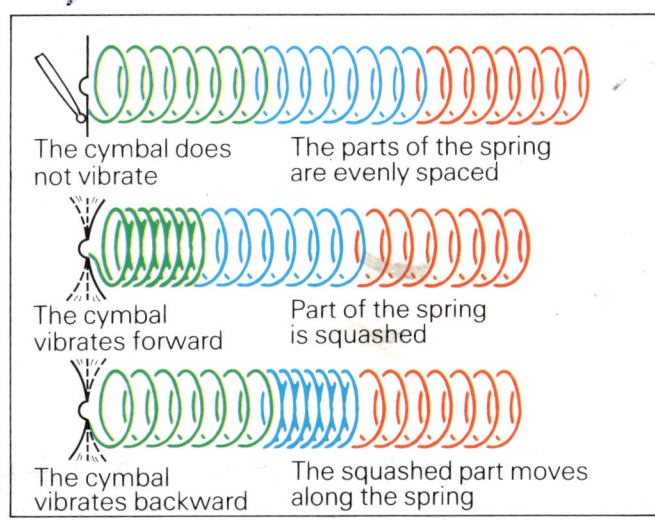

The cymbal does not vibrate	The parts of the spring are evenly spaced
The cymbal vibrates forward	Part of the spring is squashed
The cymbal vibrates backward	The squashed part moves along the spring

A sound wave moves through air by squashing and stretching it just like a spring.

at different speeds ...

When sound passes through a material the particles of which the material is made begin to vibrate. These particles pass on their vibrations to other particles. The closer the particles are to each other, the easier it is to pass on a vibration. The easier it is to pass on vibrations, the *faster* the sound passes through the material. Look at the data showing the speed of sound in different materials. Sound travels through solids better than it does through liquids or gases. When sound passes from one material to another, such as from air to water, like light it is refracted.

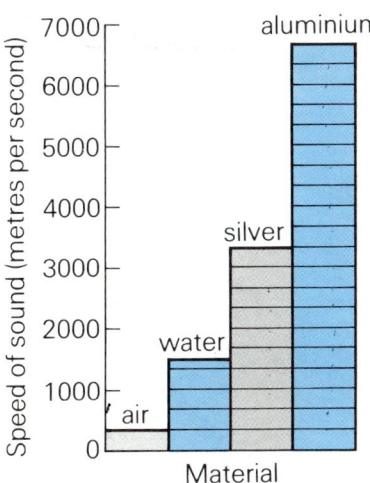

Sound travels through different materials at different speeds.

1   Name some other musical instruments that produce sound when you hit them.

2   Look at the pictures of the sound waves on the oscilloscope
  a   Which person produces the sound with the lowest frequency?
  b   Which person produces the sound with the smallest amplitude?
  c   Draw a 'picture' you would expect to see on an oscilloscope if a person with a soft deep voice talks into a microphone.

3   Why can't sound travel in an empty space (a vacuum)?

4   Refer back to spread 2 and explain the difference between a transverse wave and a longitudinal wave.

5   Look at the data on the speed of sound in different materials.
  a   Approximately how many times faster does sound travel through water compared to air?
  b   If it takes 10 seconds for sound to travel through silver, how long does it take the sound to travel the same distance through aluminium?

6 Useful sound

Sound vision

Sound, like light and other forms of waves, can be reflected (see page 6). A reflected sound wave is called an **echo**. Some animals have poor eyesight but make use of sound echoes to 'see'. This is called echolocation. Animals use very high-pitched or high-frequency sound when they use sound to 'see'. This sound is called **ultrasound** and is produced by **ultrasonic waves**. These waves can be produced by a loudspeaker connected to an electronic system such as a signal generator. The signal generator produces electrical oscillations with a wide range of frequencies. At very high frequencies, usually greater than 20 000 Hz, the waves become ultrasonic. You can't hear them, because, like the sound of a dog whistle, they are outside the range of our normal hearing.

Bats use echolocation to hunt for food and find their way in the dark.

A sound job

Ultrasound has many applications in industry. It is often used in quality control. In the examples shown here, a separate transmitter and receiver are placed opposite each other. An obstacle is positioned between the receiver and the transmitter. This interrupts the beam of ultrasound. As a result an electrical device is triggered off.

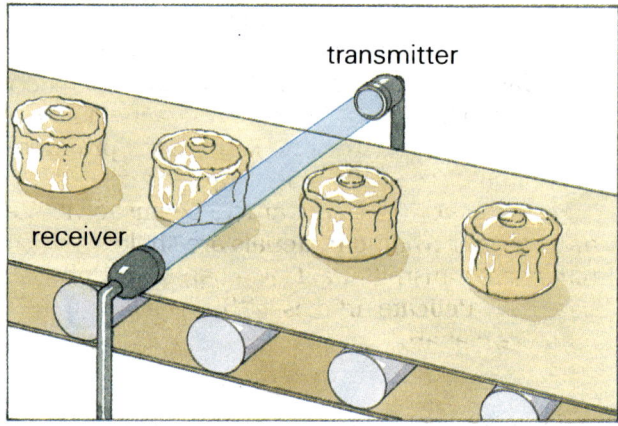

You can count automatically with ultrasound. A counter adds one to the total count of pies every time the beam is shut off.

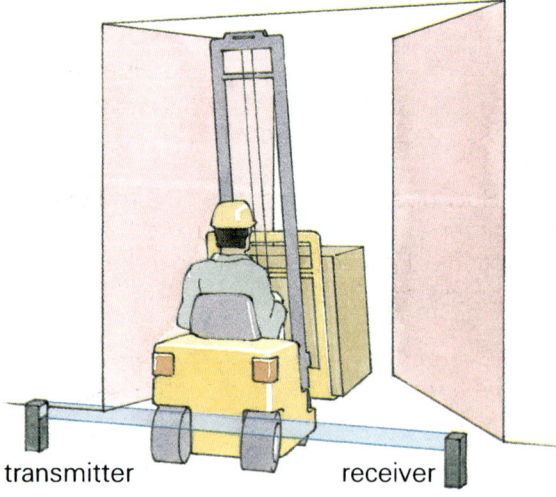

An electrical device triggers the doors to open automatically when the beam is shut off by the fork lift truck approaching.

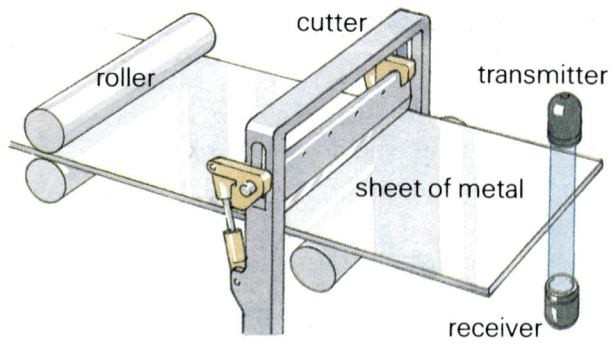

Ultrasound can be used to make sure metal sheets are cut to the right length.

Sound medicine

Ultrasonic waves and their echoes can be used to 'see' inside your body. An ultrasound transmitter is passed over the part of your body being examined. This is called **scanning**. The transmitter sends ultrasonic pulses into your body. Reflections or echoes are received from different surfaces within your body such as muscles, bones and layers of fat. The time taken for the reflections of the ultrasonic pulses to reach a detector – which is usually part of the transmitter – gives the depth within the body of the reflecting surface. The information about the time taken for different reflections is then converted into 'pictures' that you can see on a screen.

The same principle is used in industry to detect faults or flaws in metal castings. Any changes in the uniformity of the metal casting will be detected by the reflected ultrasonic pulse.

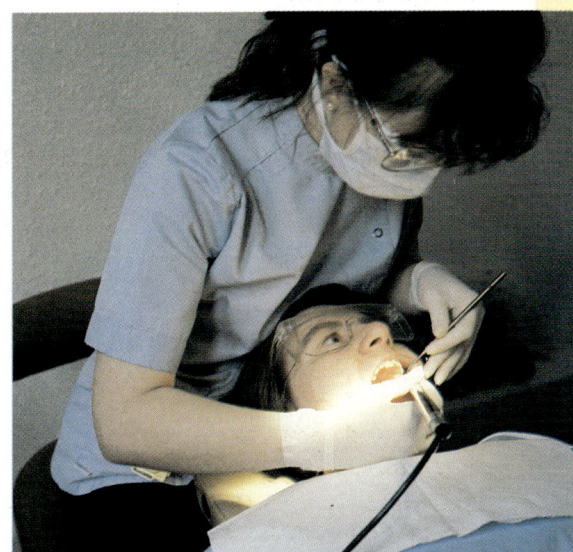

Ultrasonic sound helps mothers to 'see' their unborn babies.

Better than 'squeaky' clean

Before the vacuum cleaner became popular, small carpets were often cleaned by hanging them on a line and using a carpet beater. This technique relied on the fact that vibrations were set up in the carpet by beating it. These vibrations removed most of the dust and dirt.

The same principle is used today in **ultrasonic cleaning**. The article to be cleaned is placed in a cleaning vessel called an ultrasonic chamber. This chamber also contains an ultrasonic transmitter and a suitable solvent. This is not water but a liquid similar to the cleaning fluid used at the dry cleaners. The ultrasonic transmitter produces vibrations in the liquid. These vibrations are passed on to the article being cleaned. When the article begins to vibrate dirt, dust and other unwanted materials are shaken off. The ultrasonic transmitter acts just like the carpet beater but can clean delicate articles without having to beat them or take them apart.

Ultrasonic cleaning can be used to clean delicate articles such as jewellery, printed circuit boards and to scale and polish teeth!

1 What kinds of animals use echolocation to 'see'?

2 Explain how the use of an ultrasound beam can help make sure sheets of metal are always cut to the correct size.

3 How has ultrasound cut down the risks for a patient who doctors think might be suffering from a bad heart?

4 When a doctor wants to examine an unborn baby, what advantages does ultrasound have over X-rays?

5 How does the use of the transmitter and receiver used for ultrasound differ in its medical application and the industrial applications shown on page 12?

6 Give one reason why clothes are still cleaned with water in an automatic washing machine and not by ultrasound.

7 Radiowaves and communication

Tuned in

Next time you tune in to your favourite radio station or switch on the television for an evening's viewing, just stop and think. None of this would be possible without **radiowaves**. They belong to the same family of electromagnetic waves as light. In the same way that there are many different types of light such as red and blue, there are many different types of radiowave. Each has its own use and well-known name. Some are identified by their frequency, such as VHF or very high frequency.

Some radiowaves are identified by their wavelength – you can find long wave and medium wave on a radio.

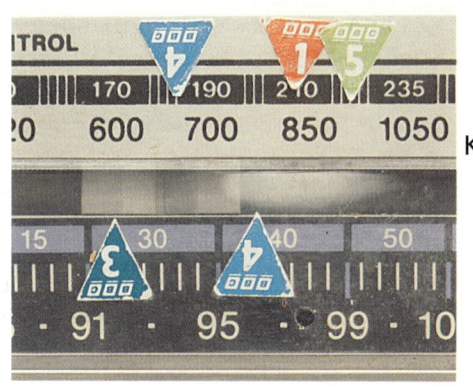

Getting the message

Transmitters at TV or radio stations send these radiowaves out across the country. The waves travel very fast – the same speed as light. A radiowave could travel from London to Manchester – a distance of about 186 miles – in just 1/1000th of a second! Unlike light, you can't see radiowaves because your eyes are not sensitive to them. You can't hear them either because like dog whistles they are outside the range of our hearing. The air, however, is literally full of them. Unlike most other forms of electromagnetic radiation, however, you don't need to worry because radiowaves have little known effect on our bodies.

The air is full of radiowaves but to be aware of them you have to be switched on and tuned in!

The message in the airways

Radiowaves can be sent or transmitted long distances in different ways, depending on their wavelength (or frequency). Radiowaves with different wavelengths have different characteristics. Those with long wavelengths can be bent or refracted like light. As a result they can follow the curvature of the Earth. This is called **ground-wave propagation** and is used for AM broadcasting and submarine communication. As the wavelength gets shorter, long distance coverage is obtained by reflecting the waves in the same way that light is reflected. They are sent upwards into the atmosphere and are reflected by a part of it called the ionosphere. This is called **sky-wave propagation**.

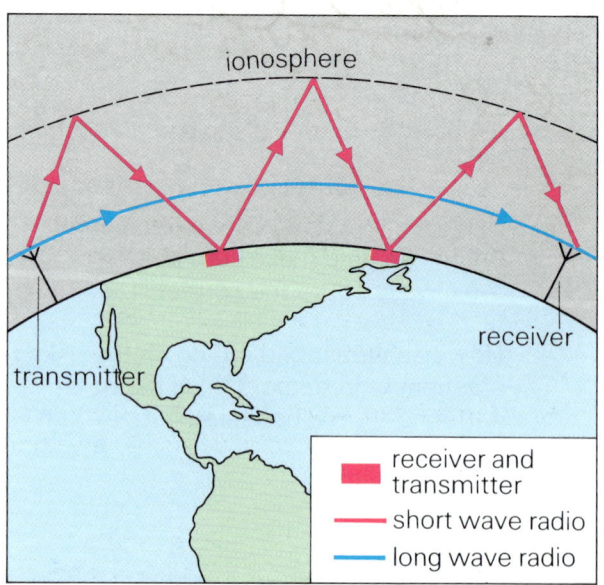

▮	receiver and transmitter
—	short wave radio
—	long wave radio

Radiowaves can be bent (refracted) or reflected long distances. Where do you think the receivers and and transmitters are sited?

The message in the sky

Radiowaves with very short wavelengths can't be bent around the Earth's surface or reflected by the ionosphere. At one time the only way to use them for communication was to position the transmitter and receiver above the Earth's horizon, so that the path of the wave would not be blocked. In this way, the transmitter could 'see' the receiver and a wave could be sent between the two in a straight line. This is called line-of-sight or **LOS propagation** and is used for television. In recent years, short wave microwaves have been used. These can pass through the ionosphere and are sent to a satellite orbiting the Earth. This collects the beam and reflects it back down to Earth.

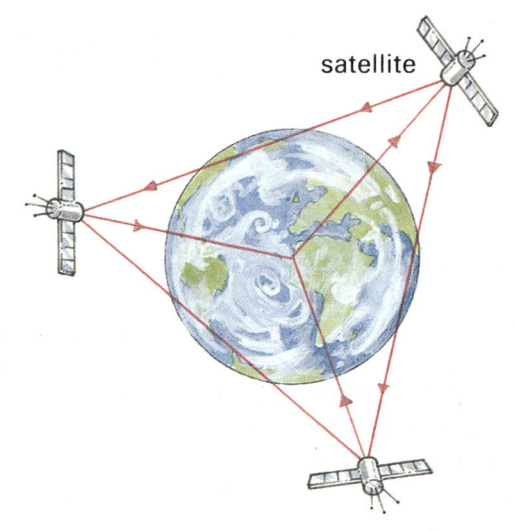

satellite

Satellites are used to reflect microwaves back to Earth or to other satellites.

Spreading the message

You may have noticed that you can pick up some AM radio signals but not others when you are travelling through a tunnel or under a bridge. Radio waves travel in straight lines so you would not expect to pick up those signals if a house or hill was between you and the transmitter. However, just as longer wavelength AM radio waves can be refracted or bent they can also be **diffracted** or spread out. The longer waves are able to spread out beyond hills and into tunnels so that you are able to pick up their signals on the aerial of your radio. An alternating current is created in the aerial with the same frequency as the radio waves. This current is then converted into sound.

Diffraction enables AM long waves to reach the parts AM medium waves cannot reach.

1 Look at the photo of the radio on the facing page. What is the approximate frequency of BBC Radios 1 and 4 in KHz?

2 How far does a radio wave travel in one second?

3 Name three ways of sending radio waves. Which one uses radio waves of very short wavelengths?

4 Draw a diagram of a reciever and a transmitter showing LOS propagation.

5 How do you know from your own experience that radio waves can travel through materials such as glass and brick?

6 What types of radio waves are reflected by satellites?

7 If you were travelling through a tunnel which AM broadcasts could you receive on your radio far better – long wave or medium wave? Explain your answer.

8 Radiation in the home

Warm or well done

Electromagnetic radiation is all around you in your home. The only sort you may be aware of is visible radiation which the eye detects as light. But there are other, invisible radiations such as **infra-red** (or IR) radiation. This radiation is given out or emitted by any hot object – even you! Electric bar fires produce IR radiation to keep you warm. The infra-red radiation is absorbed by your skin and felt as heat. The same radiation is produced by grills, ovens and toasters for cooking, as well as remote controls for TV sets and VCRs.

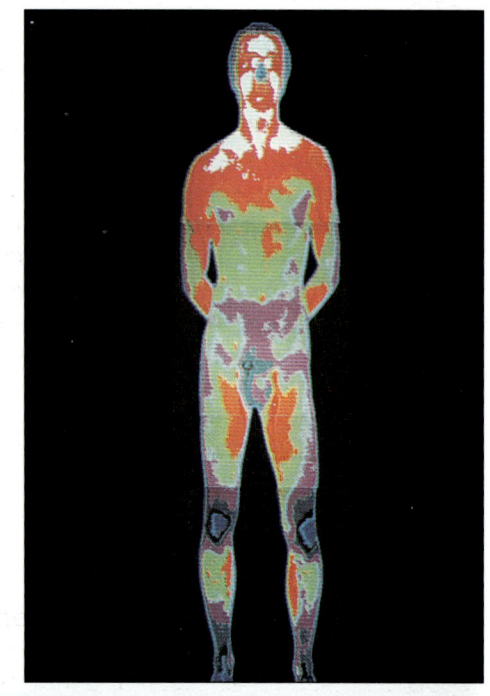

Special photographic film can be used to show that you emit IR radiation – black denotes no radiation, and purple, blue, green, red and white denote increasing amounts of radiation in the form of heat.

Chasing the UV

Some people go on holiday to lie on the beach for a couple of weeks and come back home with a sun tan. They might be said to be 'chasing the Sun'. In reality, they are chasing **ultra-violet** (UV) radiation from the Sun. A good sun tan is produced by gradual and careful exposure to the UV radiation in the Sun's rays. However, the Sun is not the only source of UV radiation people use to become sun tanned. Some people will go to great lengths to have a tan all the year round! . . .

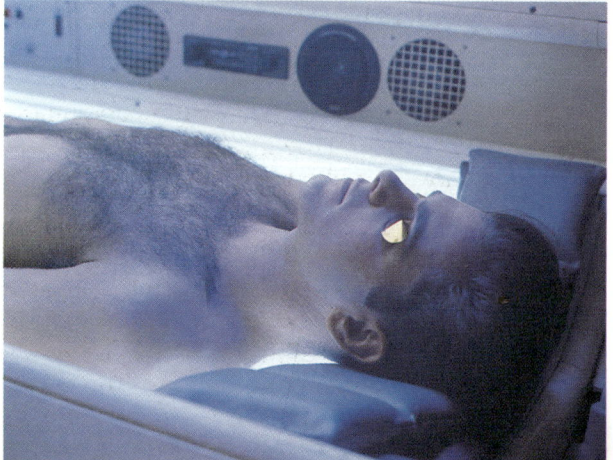

Sunbeds produce UV radiation which can give you an artificial sun tan.

Skin-deep protection

Very few people grumble when the weather is warm and sunny. However, all forms of radiation, including UV radiation from the Sun, can cause damage to living cells. If you receive too much UV radiation it can damage your skin cells and this can cause skin cancer. To stop this from happening, your skin acts as a protective barrier by reflecting some of the radiation. Your body also produces a pigment or colouring called melanin to protect the living cells even more. This makes your skin darker. The more radiation you receive, the more melanin your body produces so the darker your skin becomes. The darker your skin, the more radiation it absorbs. This means less UV radiation reaches the living cells beneath the skin.

People who have evolved in areas of intense sunlight, such as Africa and Australia, have more melanin in their skin.

Being smart

Some substances are able not only to absorb UV and other forms of radiation, but also to emit some of the energy absorbed as light. Perhaps the best known examples of this occurring in nature are the glow-worm and the firefly. The same principle is used in fluorescent lamps. The lamp emits UV radiation. The inside of the lamp is coated with a chemical which absorbs the UV radiation and converts it into visible light. You also behave like a glow-worm or firefly in UV light. To be more exact, some of your clothes emit light. This is because washing powders contain chemicals called 'brightening agents'. These brightening agents absorb UV radiation then emit it as light so the clothes look brighter. This phenomenon is known as **fluorescence**. Fluorescence is also used to protect against fraud. Many building society books have signatures written in invisible ink containing a fluorescent substance which will show up in UV light.

Brightening agents added to washing powders make clothes look even whiter.

Cookability – by microwave

Microwaves are more penetrating than IR radiation. They are able to pass through the surface of food to a depth of about 5 cm. Microwave ovens are specially tuned – just like you'd tune your radio – so that the microwaves they produce are absorbed by water, which all foods contain. The energy from the microwave radiation is transferred to the water molecules. This causes them to move about more and so produce more heat. This heat is then conducted to the centre of the food in the same way as cooking with gas or electricity – but the heat now has less distance to travel, making the food cook faster!

Some microwave ovens often fail to cook food evenly to a safe enough temperature (about 70°C) to kill harmful bacteria such as salmonella. To get over this problem, you can now buy microwave ovens fitted with a temperature probe which measures the temperature at the centre of the food. The oven switches itself off only when this temperature has been reached.

IR radiation used in a grill is converted to heat energy which cooks the food

A probe measures the temperature at the centre of the food to make sure all the harmful bacteria have been killed

1　State three uses of infra-red radiation

2　What type of radiation is used in sunbeds?

3　How does microwave radiation cook food?

4　Why can too much ultra-violet radiation be harmful?

5　What is fluorescence and how is it used?

6　What are the different effects of infra-red and UV radiation on the skin?

9 Natural radiation

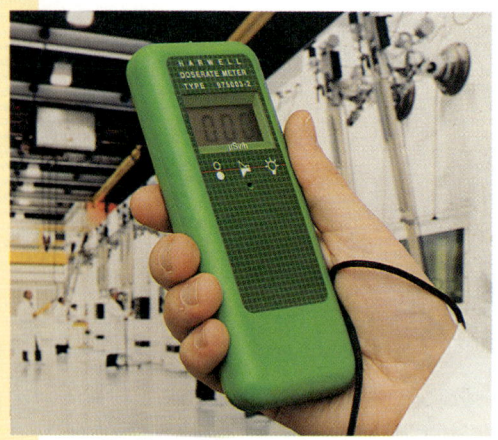

Radioactivity can be detected using a Geiger counter – the needle moves on the scale to show how radioactive the material is.

What is meant by radioactive?

You will already be familiar with some sorts of radiation, such as the rays from the Sun. Not only do these allow you to see but they also keep you warm. There is another form of radiation that we cannot see or feel. This arises because all materials contain energy. Some materials release some of this energy as invisible radiation – they are said to be **radioactive**.

Where does radiation come from?

The radiation from radioactive materials is all around us. Most of what you receive comes from four main sources:

● *Outer space* – This comes from the Sun, our galaxy and possibly other galaxies. It is called **cosmic radiation**. The further away you are from the Earth's surface, the more cosmic radiation you receive.

● *The air* – Air contains two radioactive gases called radon and thoron. These are produced by two other radioactive elements thorium and uranium which are found naturally in the Earth. This type of radiation could be a problem in poorly ventilated mines.

● *Rocks and soil* – Some materials in rocks and soil are naturally radioactive. Coal, for example, contains small amounts of natural radioactive materials such as uranium and radium. We use some of the rocks to make building materials.

● *Food and drink* – Natural radioactive material on the Earth's surface is taken up by plants and animals and becomes dissolved in water.

Radiation from radioactive materials is all around you – even in the food you eat.

How much radioactivity do you receive?

You measure the amount of pocket money you receive each year in pounds, the basic unit of money. The amount of radiation you receive each year (or the radiation dose) is measured in a basic unit called the **millisievert**. The total amount of radiation you receive from all sources is about 2.5 units. A very large dose of radiation would be greater than 1000 units. Most of the radiation you receive comes from natural sources, as you can see in the picture. Which is the largest source of radiation?

How much radiation do you receive from other sources?

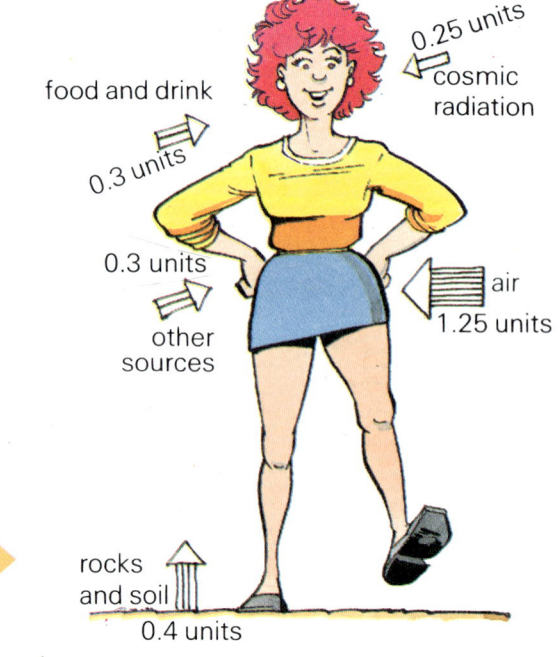

food and drink
0.3 units

0.25 units
cosmic radiation

0.3 units
other sources

air
1.25 units

rocks and soil
0.4 units

Other sources of radiation

Although natural radiation has been here since the Earth was formed, other sources have increased greatly in the last 100 years. The amount of radiation you receive from these other sources each year is about 0.3 units.

The largest source of non-natural radiation is in the field of medicine. Most of us have had an X-ray at some time. A typical chest X-ray gives you about 0.02 or 1/50th of a unit of radioactivity.

Another source of radiation in recent times is from nuclear power stations. They use energy released by radioactive materials such as uranium to produce electricity. A major accident in a nuclear power station such as that at Chernobyl in 1986 can result in radioactive materials being released into the atmosphere. This is called **radioactive fallout**.

Radioactive fallout has also been produced by the use of nuclear weapons. The first atomic bombs were dropped on Hiroshima and Nagasaki in 1945. Since then nuclear weapons have been tested above ground in the 1950s and 1960s. The graph shows that the amount of radioactive fallout has decreased considerably in recent years despite further testing. Can you suggest a reason why?

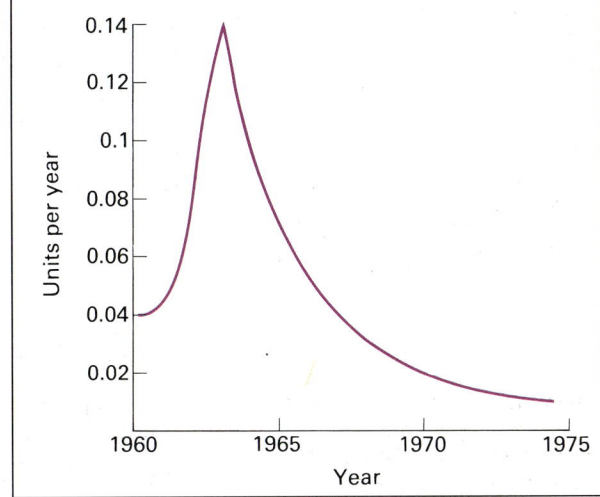

The amount of radioactive fallout varied considerably during the 1960s and 1970s.

Activity – human and radio!

The lives people lead mean that some receive more than the average amount of radioactivity in one year. Look at the picture and work out which person receives a higher dose of cosmic rays. Which person receives a higher dose of X-rays? Which person could receive radiation from thoron and uranium? Can you think of reasons why this should be so?

Some occupations receive more radiation than others.

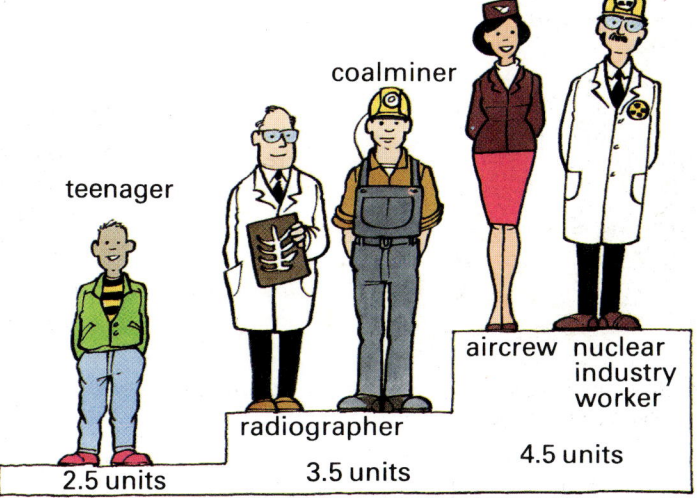

teenager
2.5 units

radiographer
3.5 units

coalminer

aircrew nuclear industry worker
4.5 units

1 How is the radiation from radioactive materials **a** different from, and **b** similar to radiation from the Sun?

2 Name five radioactive materials mentioned in the text.

3 **a** Convert the information given about the amounts of radiation from different sources into a pie chart.
   b What 'other sources' of radiation are there, apart from these natural sources?

4 Look at the graph.
   a In what year was the radioactive fallout the highest?
   b Redraw the graph to show what you think it might look like from 1940.

5 Explain why a person living in a draught-proof house might receive in one year more than the average radiation dose.

6 Do you think it's more sensible to live in a coastal region liable to flooding than at high altitude?

10 The best radiation for the job

Different properties – different uses

There are three different types of radiation emitted or given out by radioactive materials. These are called **alpha** (α), **beta** (β) and **gamma** (γ) radiation. Alpha and beta radiation consist of different types of particles. Gamma radiation is electromagnetic radiation, like light, but a much more energetic form.

The three types of radiation emitted by radioactive sources have different penetrating powers.

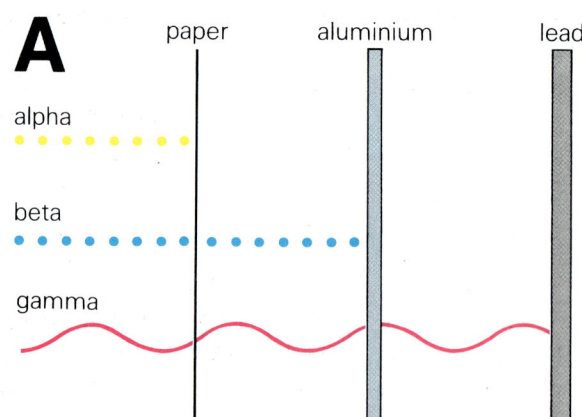

A   paper   aluminium   lead

alpha

beta

gamma

The three different types of radiation have different properties. One of these properties is their ability to pass through some materials. This is called their penetrating power. Look at the diagram above. Which type of radiation is the most penetrating?

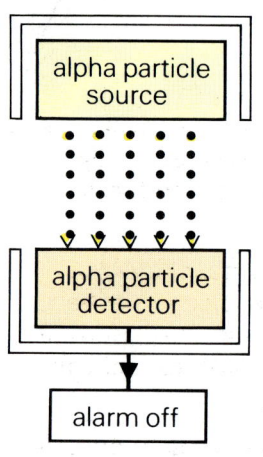

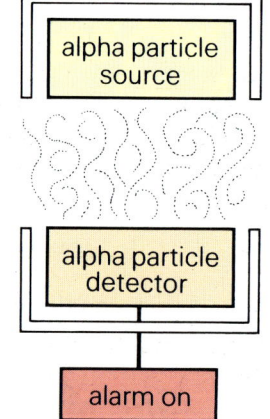

(a) *The alarm stays off as long as the detector receives alpha particles.*

(b) *The alpha particles can't penetrate the smoke – the detector doesn't receive alpha particles so the alarm sounds.*

Smoke alarms

Each year hundreds of people die and thousands are injured in fires in their own home. Many of these deaths could have been prevented if people had been able to escape from the fire before it was too late. Smoke alarms placed in the correct place are able to give you more time to escape from a fire. They make use of the fact that alpha particles are not very penetrating. The diagrams show you how a smoke alarm works. Why do you think that beta and gamma particles are unsuitable for use in smoke alarms?

Through thick . . . and thin

Radiation can also be used by industry to check the thicknesses of different types of materials – for example in metal rolling or paper making. A radiation detector such as a Geiger–Müller tube is used to collect radiation which has passed through a material. The Geiger–Müller tube is connected to a counter. This counts the amount of radiation passing through the material. If the amount or 'count' remains the same it means that the thickness of the material has not changed. A decrease in the count means that less radiation is being detected, so that the material is getting thicker. What does an increase in the count mean?

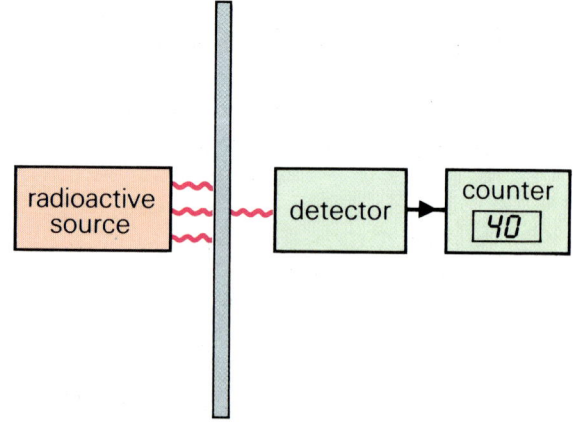

Gamma rays can pass through sheet metal and can be used to detect its thickness.

Down to the bone

Radiations from radioactive materials are not the only types that are useful because of their penetrating powers. X-rays are another form of radiation but they are produced by machines, not radioactive materials. They are a form of highly energetic electromagnetic radiation, like gamma rays. They also pass through some substances more easily than others and are just as penetrating as gamma rays.

The penetrating powers of X-rays are used in medicine to help doctors see what's going on inside the body. X-rays do not pass as easily through some parts of the body, particularly bones, as they do through flesh. If X-rays are fired at the body, some will pass through and can be detected as a dark image on photographic film. Bones and other dense parts show up as white areas on the film, as only a few X-rays passed through and were detected.

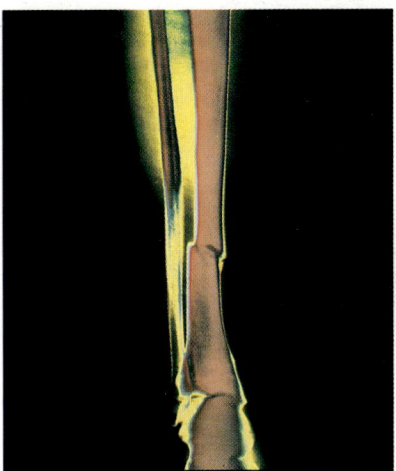

The film produces a shadow picture of bones because X-rays will not pass through them.

Destroying harmful cells

When radiation from radioactive materials and from X-rays penetrates substances, some of it strikes atoms in the substances and the atoms become electrically charged. These electrically charged atoms are called **ions**. The radiation which produces these ions is sometimes called **ionising** radiation.

This radiation can penetrate cells, which are the building blocks of all living matter. When it does so it can cause changes in the cells. Some of these changes damage or kill off the cells. Harmful cells inside our bodies which cause cancer can be killed by gamma radiation.

There are also bacterial cells in the air around us. Some are harmful and if they get inside our bodies, for example during an operation, they can grow and cause disease. Instruments used for operations are sterilised by exposing them to gamma radiation to kill these bacteria.

Some foods can be irradiated to keep them fresh by killing harmful bacteria. Untreated food will quickly rot.

1 Redraw diagram A to include the penetrating power of X-rays.

2 a Why must the distance between an alpha particle source and its detector be very short?
  b Name two parts of the home unsuitable for placing smoke detectors.

3 What type of radiation can be used to check the thickness of sheets of **a** metal, and **b** paper? Give reasons for your answer.

4 In what ways are X-rays **a** similar to, and **b** different from, gamma rays?

5 Gamma rays may be used to take pictures of metal tanks or boilers to check for cracks. Explain how this works.

6 Harmful cancer cells which begin to grow rapidly form a tumour. Why is treatment using gamma rays directed only at the tumour and not at other parts of the body?

11 *The risks of radiation*

What does radiation do... ⬦

Radiation from X-rays and from radioactive materials can be very useful (see pages 20–1). But radiation can also be harmful. Before such risks were understood, workers were employed to paint luminous figures on watch and clock dials. The paint contained a radioactive material called radium. It was found that many of these workers died at an early age. Other studies have been done on the effects of radiation. By far the largest study is of the survivors of the two nuclear bombs dropped on Hiroshima and Nagasaki towards the end of the Second World War. This again showed that some of these people died at a much earlier age when compared to the rest of the Japanese population.

The larger the dose of radiation, the greater the risk of damage to your health.

Dose received	Effect
2.5 units	You receive about this much each year, and are still healthy.
1000 units	A large dose like this in a short time can cause vomiting and skin burns
10 000 units	A very large dose can be fatal

... outside the body? ⬦

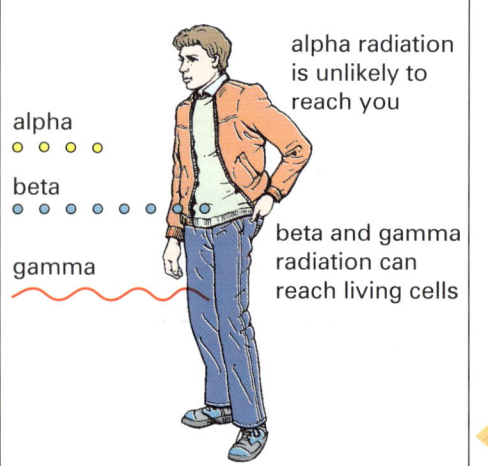

alpha radiation is unlikely to reach you

alpha

beta

gamma

beta and gamma radiation can reach living cells

You are made of many millions of cells. Some of these die every day and are replaced by new ones. Sometimes cells can become faulty and they start to multiply at a much faster rate than usual. These rapidly multiplying cells are called cancer cells. They quickly replace other normal cells so that parts of your body stop working properly. Cancer cells can occur without radiation. However, people exposed to large doses of beta and gamma radiation have a greater possibility of getting cancer – just like people who are exposed to smoking run a greater risk of getting lung cancer. Very large doses of radiation can kill living cells – so many cells that your body cannot replace them fast enough and will eventually die.

Outside the body beta and gamma radiation are the most dangerous.

... inside the body? ⬦

Gamma rays have similar penetrating powers to X-rays (see pages 20–1). Similar precautions must be taken to avoid exposure to them. Alpha and beta radiation do not penetrate very far into your body (spread 10) so that the risk to your health from materials that give out these types of radiation is very small. However, radioactive substances can contaminate the food that you eat or the air that you breath. Once inside your body, alpha radiation can also kill normal healthy cells. To reduce the risk of this happening, no eating, drinking or smoking is allowed where any radioactive materials are being handled.

All radiation is dangerous inside your body but alpha radiation is the most dangerous.

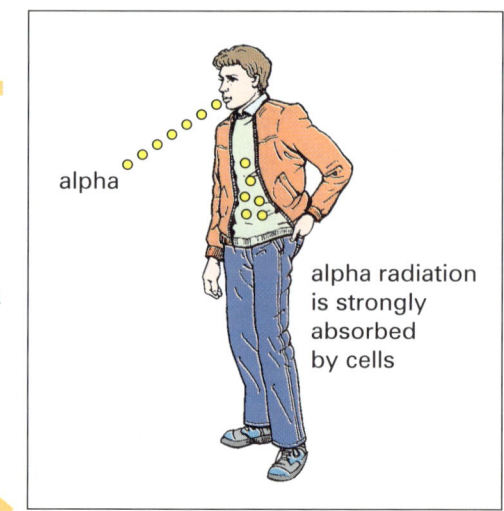

alpha

alpha radiation is strongly absorbed by cells

Minimising the risks

No radiation dose, however small, can be assumed to be entirely free of risk. Because of this, all exposures to radiation should be made as low as possible. As you have learned, X-rays can't penetrate through lead. Radiographers, when operating X-ray machines, stop X-rays from getting to them by working behind a screen containing lead. The small amount of radiation they do receive is measured at regular intervals to make sure it is within safe limits. Care is also taken to protect the patients. The equipment is surrounded by lead to make sure X-rays don't escape and patients sometimes wear lead gowns. Only in very special circumstances are X-rays given to pregnant women, in case the radiation damages the baby.

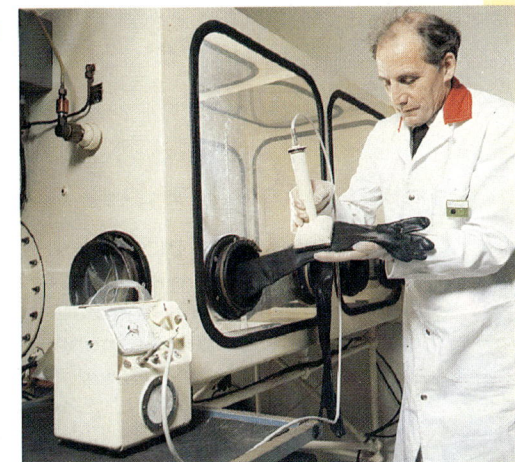

The dose to radiation workers is monitored by film badges and other types of detector.

For how long?

When a substance emits radiation, its unstable atoms change into a different kind of atom. This process is called **radioactive decay**. You can detect the radiation emitted and count how much is being produced in a certain time. If you plot your results on a graph you obtain a **decay curve**. The time taken for the number of counts to fall by half is called the **half life**($t_{\frac{1}{2}}$). The half life is always the same value for a particular atom. From the decay curve opposite you can see that for radon gas the half life is a constant value of about 50 seconds. When radioactive substances are used in medicine, they should have a short half life so that any material remaining in the body quickly decays away.

During one half life, the number radioactive atoms has been halved. This means, in practice, that during this time the mass of the radioactive substance decreases by half.

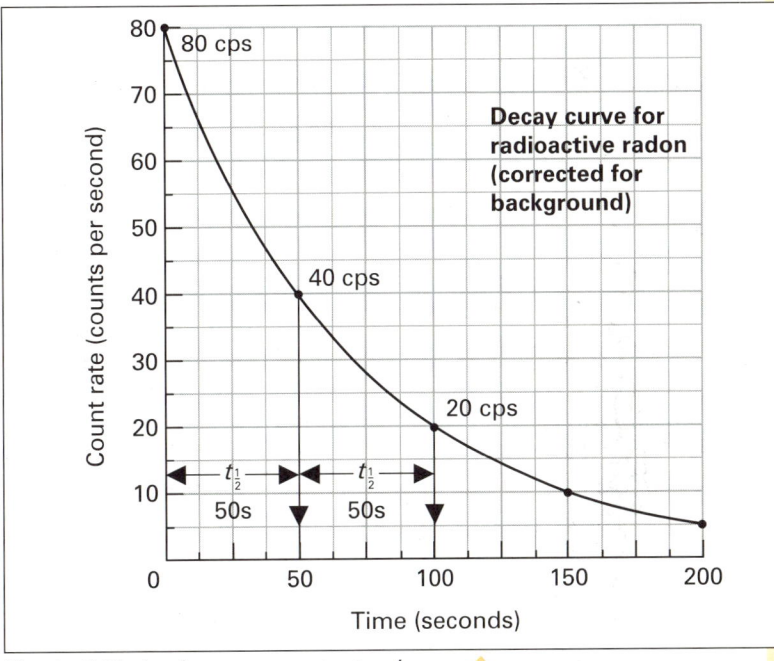

The half life is always a constant value.

1. Give two examples of workers who suffered harm as a result of exposure to radiation.

2. How much radiation needs to be received before a person suffers from skin burns?

3. What precautions do radiographers take to avoid exposure to X-rays?

4. What safety precautions should be observed when working in an area where radioactive substances are being used?

5. Look at the decay curve for radon. What would the count be after 200 seconds? How long would it take for the count to fall to zero?

6. A 12 g sample of radioactive substance has a half life of 8 years. How much of the sample would remain after 24 years?

12 Radioactive substances

Inside the atom

Everything on Earth, including you, is made up of tiny particles or atoms. The atom was found to be made up of three basic sub-atomic particles: protons, neutrons and electrons. in 1911, to explain the results of experiments, a scientist called Rutherford proposed the following model for the atom.

At the centre of the atom is a nucleus which contains protons and neutrons. The electrons orbit the nucleus in much the same way that planets in our solar system orbit the Sun. Experiments also revealed information about the relative mass and charge of these particles. This information is summarised in the table opposite. The number of protons and electrons inside an atom is always the same so that it has no overall charge.

Sub-atomic particle	Mass	Charge
proton	1	+1
neutron	1	0
electron	negligible	−1

Protons and neutrons have the same mass. Protons and electrons have equal but opposite charges.

Element	Atomic number
hydrogen	1
helium	2
lithium	3
beryllium	4
boron	5
carbon	6
nitrogen	7

Types of atoms

Not all atoms are the same: different kinds of atom have different numbers of protons, neutrons and electrons. The type of atom, however, is determined only by the number of protons found inside the nucleus. All atoms which have the same number of protons belong to the same **element**. The number of protons in an atom of an element is called its **atomic number** or **proton number**.

Elements are identified by their atomic number.

Isotopes

The protons and neutrons found at the centre of the atom are together referred to as **nucleons** – particles that belong to the nucleus. The total mass of an atom depends almost entirely on the number of protons and neutrons in its nucleus – electrons have hardly any mass. The number of protons and neutrons in an atom of an element is therefore called its **mass number** or **nucleon number**.

Sometimes two atoms of an element have the same number of protons or atomic number but a different number of neutrons. These atoms have different mass numbers. Atoms of an element with the same atomic number but different mass number are called **isotopes**. The diagram shows you two isotopes of the element helium.

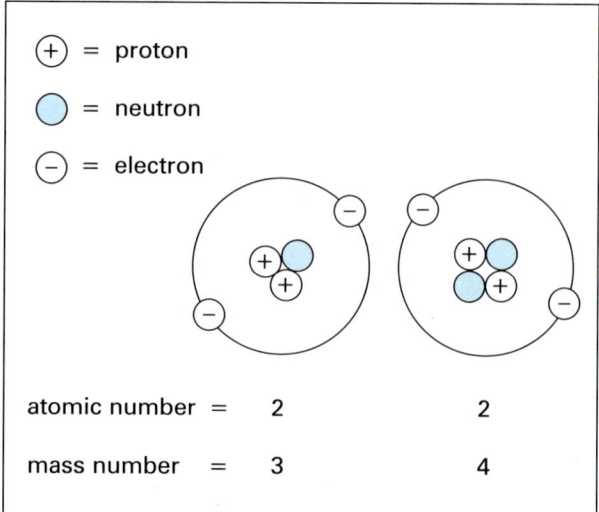

Isotopes have the same number of protons but different numbers of neutrons.

Radioactive isotopes

Most isotopes are stable but a few have nuclei that are unstable. A nucleus seems to be stable if it has the right balance of protons and neutrons. If a nucleus is unstable it has too many or too few neutrons and it is likely to split up or disintegrate. If an unstable nucleus of an isotope breaks up, the isotope is said to be **radioactive**. Any isotope of an element that is radioactive is called a **radioisotope** (or radionuclide). When a nucleus breaks up it is said to decay so that the process is often referred to as **radioactive decay** (see page 23). When a nucleus breaks up it gives out radiation. The diagram opposite shows that there are two different types of radiation given out or emitted by radioactive substances. The older a piece of radioactive material is, the less radiation it emits. This idea can be used to date materials.

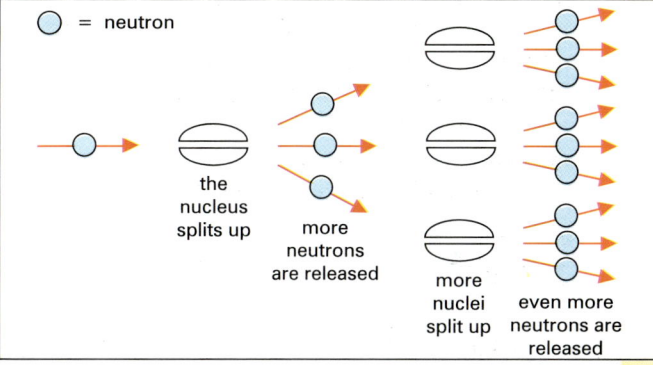

Both alpha and beta radioactive decay produce a new atom with a different number of protons to the original atom.

Nuclear fuel

For many years fossil fuels such as coal and oil have been used to provide the heat needed to produce steam for turbines in power stations. These turbines help to generate electricity. Nuclear power stations work on the same principle as coal or oil fired power stations but nuclear fuel instead of fossil fuel is used to generate the heat.

The neutrons released in nuclear fission may cause a chain reaction.

Uranium is the fuel used in most nuclear power stations. The nucleus of a uranium atom can capture a neutron and split into smaller nuclei. This splitting of a nucleus is called **nuclear fission**. The two new products formed, called fission products, are themselves unstable and emit radiation. Two or three very fast moving neutrons are also produced in the fission process and, as the diagram opposite shows, they may start a **chain reaction**. Uranium can be used as a fuel because very large amounts of energy are released in this process. Approximately twenty thousand times as much energy is released from uranium by the process of nuclear fission as is released by the same amount of carbon and oxygen combining to release energy by chemical bond formation when coal is burned.

1 What is meant by the following words: atomic number, mass number, nucleon, radioactive, nuclear fission?

2
a Name the three particles found inside the nucleus of an atom.
b Which particle is the lightest?
c Which particle has no charge?

3
a What is the atomic number of the element helium?
b Which element has atomic number 5?

4 The element lithium has an atomic number of 3? It exists as two isotopes with atomic numbers 6 and 7.

a How many protons, neutrons and electrons does each isotope contain?
b Draw a model of each isotope.

5 An atom X with a mass number of 224 and an atomic number of 88 decays by emitting alpha particles. What is the mass number and atomic number of the new atom formed?

6 If the energy released from burning 1 kg of coal warms a room for 2 hours, how long (in years) would the energy released by the fission of the same amount of uranium warm the room for?'

13 Seismic waves

The Earth's structure

The average diameter of the Earth is about 12 750 km but our attempts to find direct evidence about its inside have barely scratched the surface. The bottoms of the deepest mines are less than 4 km down. Geologists have drilled different parts of the Earth's crust but the depth to which they go rarely exceeds 10 km. This means the vast bulk of the Earth's interior remains untouched and must be investigated by other less direct methods. The most important of these methods are seismic waves associated with earthquakes and explosions.

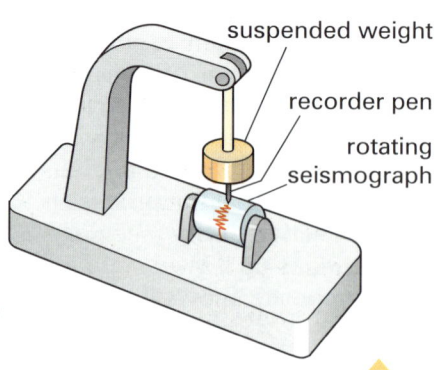

suspended weight
recorder pen
rotating seismograph

A simple seismometer records vibrations set up by earthquakes.

Shock waves

Earthquakes and explosions cause sudden releases of vast amounts of energy. The energy released causes vibrations in the particles that make up the body of the Earth. These vibrations travel through the Earth as a series of waves called **shock waves** or **seismic waves**.

Two types of shock waves travel through the body of the Earth: **P** or primary waves and **S** or secondary waves. In P waves the particles vibrate backwards and forwards in the direction along which the wave is travelling. Like sound waves, they are longitudinal waves. In S waves the particles vibrate in a direction at right angles to the direction in which the wave is travelling. Like light waves, they are transverse waves.

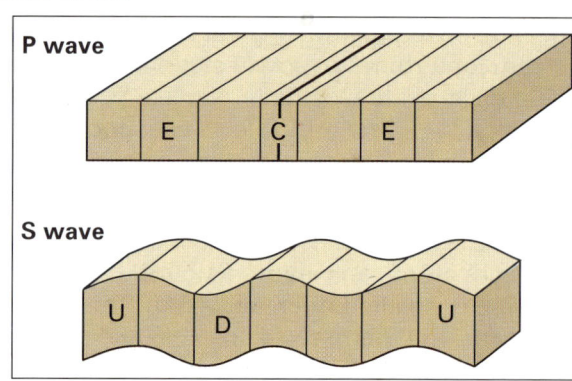

Rocks are compressed (C) and extended (E) by a P wave, shaken up (U) and down (D) by an S wave.

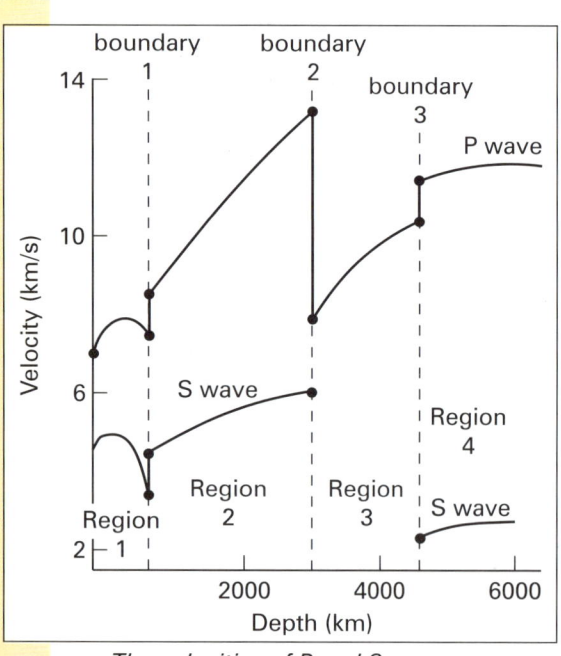

The velocities of P and S waves in the body of the Earth.

Shock wave velocities

The change in the velocities of shock waves gives us useful information about the internal structure of the Earth. In general, the closer together particles are, the easier it is for a particle to pass on to its neighbouring particle vibrations from shock waves. This means that denser materials such as solids, which have particles closer together, will have greater shock wave velocities than liquid materials which are less dense.

The graph opposite shows how the velocities of P and S waves change in the body of the Earth.

Notice that:

● P waves travel faster than S waves

● S waves don't travel in liquids, therefore region 3 is a liquid

● There is a sudden increase or decrease in velocity at three places identified as boundaries.

Wave paths

The change in velocity of waves as they travel through the body of the Earth is caused by the waves passing through denser material in the same region. It is also caused by the waves moving through the boundaries between the different regions. The change in velocity of the wave causes it to change direction or bend. The bending of a wave is called **refraction**. You have already read about refraction of water, light and sound waves (pages 6–9, 11).

The diagram shows the path of P waves through the body of the Earth. Region 1 is the **crust** and is too thin to be included. Region 2 is the **mantle**, a very syrupy or viscous liquid. The refraction of the wave in the mantle shows that the density of the mantle increases with increase in depth. Region 3 is the **outer core** which is made up of a liquid. Region 4 is the **inner core** which is solid. The waves paths are refracted within each particular layer, showing that there is a change of density within each layer. The greatest amount of refraction, however, occurs at the boundaries between layers. This shows that there are large differences in the density and hence type of material found in each layer.

wave source

Region 4

Region 3

Region 2

▲ *P waves are refracted when they pass through the body of the Earth.*

1 What causes shock waves? How are they detected?

2 State two differences between an S wave and a P wave.

3
a What is refraction?
b State two reasons for the refraction of P waves within the body of the Earth.

4 Which part of the Earth's internal structure is
a the thinnest
b made up of liquid?

5 Look at the graph showing the wave velocities.
a Identify each region as core, crust or mantle.
b What are the velocities of S and P waves at a depth of 2000 km?
c Why is the velocity of P waves in Region 2 greater than their velocity in Region 3?

6 Look at the path of P waves. Why do the waves travel in curved paths within a region but change direction abruptly between regions?

14 The radiation band

More than just a name

There is more to the family of radiant energy than just a name. Like any family, each member has its own individual characteristics. Radiation is characterised by its frequency and wavelength. The properties of the waves – such as the amount of energy they transfer and their ability to be reflected or pass through materials – depend on their frequency and wavelength.

Different properties of radiant energy can be put to different uses.

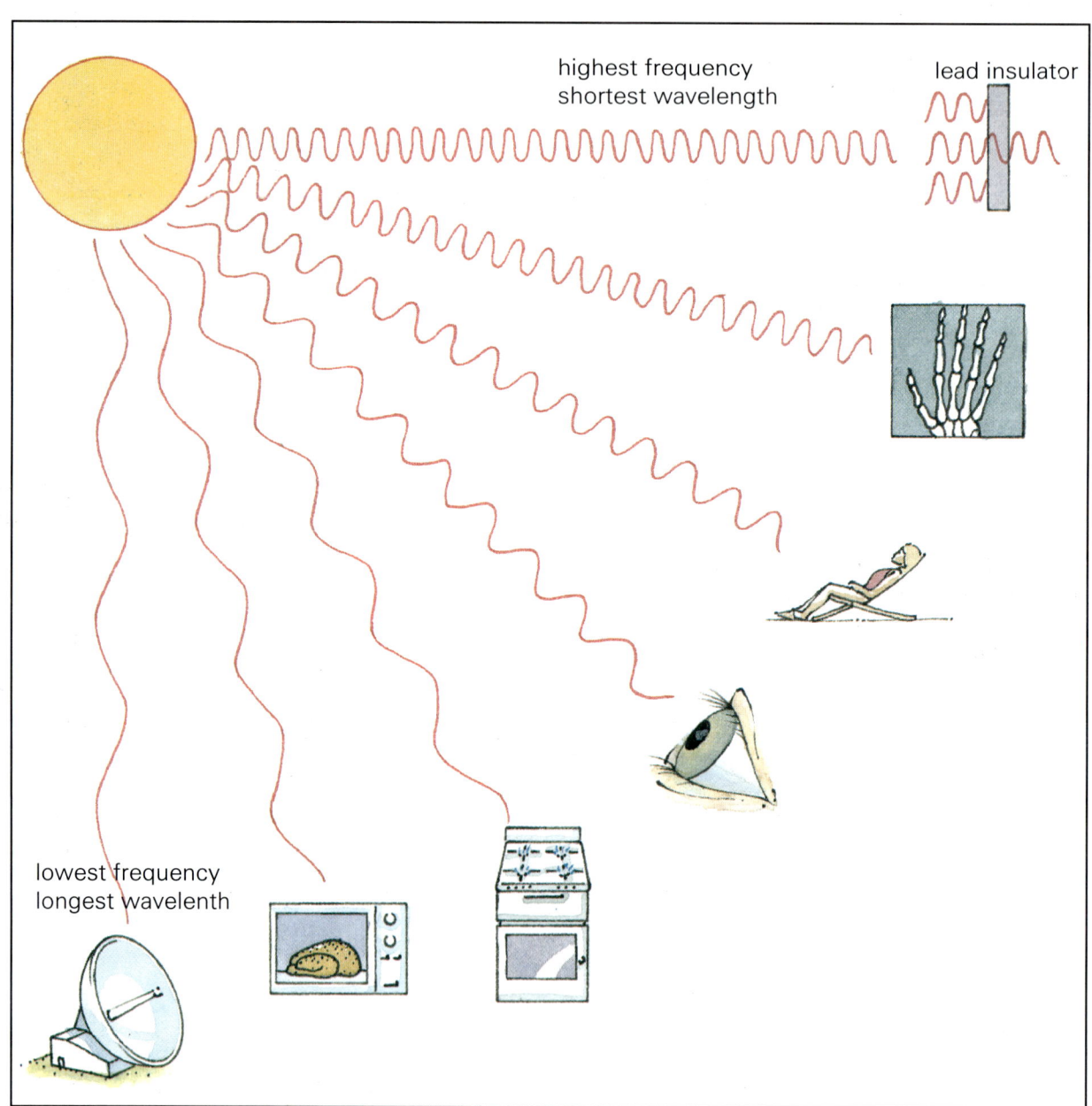

highest frequency
shortest wavelength

lead insulator

lowest frequency
longest wavelenth

Spreading the name

Waves have other special properties. You can hear someone talking to you on the other side of an open door even if you are not standing directly in front of it. You can even hear someone shouting at you from the other side of the building. You can hear these sounds because when sound waves – or any other waves – meet an obstacle or pass through a gap they spread out from the edges or corners. This ability of waves to spread out round corners is called **diffraction** (see page 15).

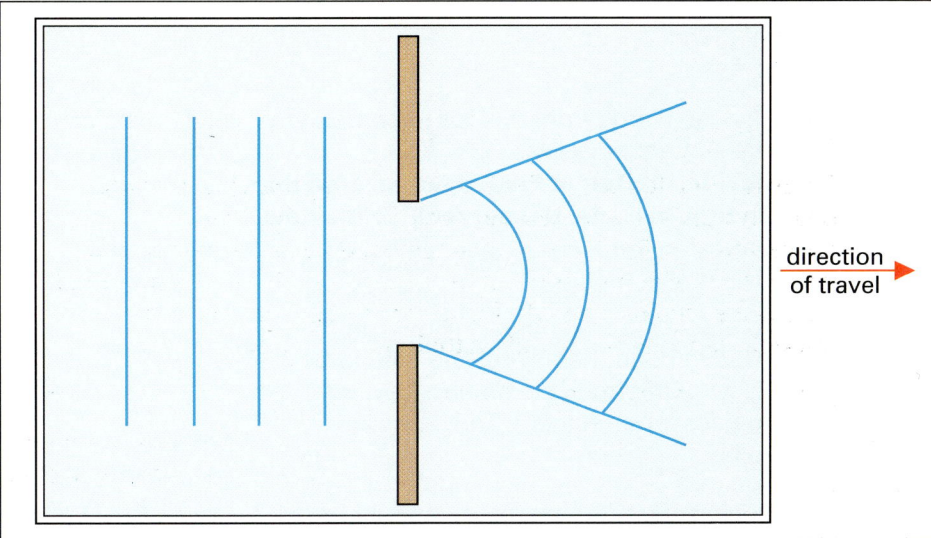

When the width of the gap in the barrier is comparable to the wavelength of the waves, the extent of the diffraction is large.

The diagrams show you what happens to straight waves in a ripple tank when they have to pass through a gap. The diagrams show that the waves have started to become circular in shape and are also starting to spread out or diffract. The extent of the diffraction depends on the relationship between the width of the gap and the wavelength of the wave.

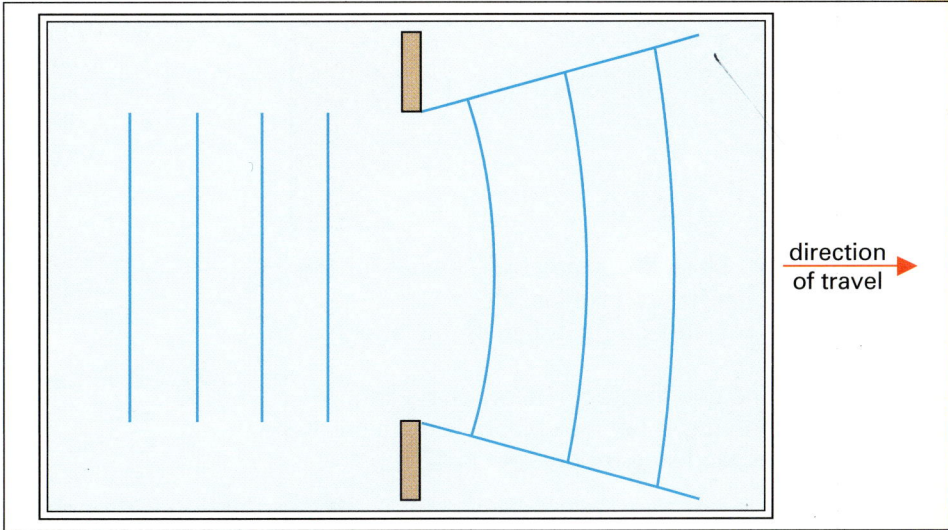

When the width of the gap in the barrier is greater than the wavelength of the waves, the extent of diffraction is small.

1 Identify each type of radiation in the picture on page 28, and name one property of each type that is needed by the particular use illustrated.

2 Arrange the different types of radiation in order of:
  a increasing frequency
  b increasing wavelength.

3 State two properties that all electromagnetic radiations have in common.

4 What affect if any does each type of radiation have on living cells.

5 Give one example of the deflection of sound.

6 Sound and water waves are not the only waves that can be diffracted. Electromagnetic radiation, such as light, can also be diffracted. What are the similarities and differences between sound waves and electromagnetic waves?

1 Choose words from this list to complete the sentences below.

liquids, matter, curved, opaque, straight, energy, particle, transparent, solid, wave

Light travels in .... lines. It travels as a wave which transfers ...... from one place to another. Some objects allow light to pass through them. They are said to be .... Other objects do not allow light to pass through them. They are said to be ....

2 This diagram shows part of a red, rear perspex reflector on a bicycle.
a What is the effect at X and Y called?

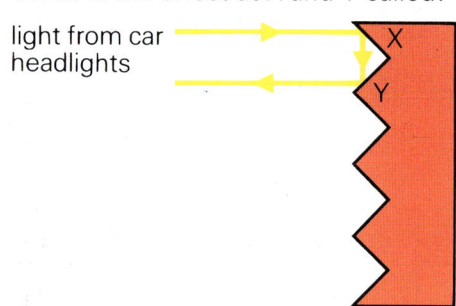

light from car headlights

b State two conditions needed for this effect to take place.
c State one other use of this effect.

3 The two diagrams below show light entering a perspex block. The critical angle of incidence for perspex is 42°.

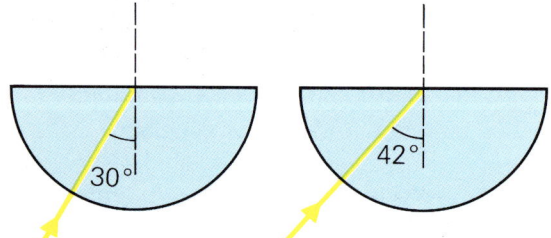

30°   42°

Complete the path of light through each glass block.

4 The cardboard box shown is used to store radioactive material.

DANGER

a Which radioactive source could be stored in the box?
b Name one use of this type of radioactivity.
c Why are radioactive materials dangerous?
d You would see the danger signal (i) at which hospital department? (ii) at which type of power station?
e A detector placed in the cardboard box still recorded 30 counts in 10 seconds with no radioactive source in the box. What is the count rate in counts per second?
f State two possible sources of this radiation.

5 A sample of igneous rock contains very small amounts of uranium. Over a period of time, the uranium decays to lead. The relative amounts of uranium and lead isotopes can be used to date the rock. The decay curve for uranium is shown below.
a What is the half life of uranium?
b If the relative proportions of lead and uranium in a rock sample were found to be 52% and 48% respectively, how old is the rock?

Relative % of uranium compared to lead

100
90
80
70
60
50
40
30
20
10
0   1 2 3 4 5 6 7 8

Time ($\times 10^9$ years)

Some students were investigating the amount of noise produced by different aircraft by looking at the 'picture' of the sound produced on an oscilloscope. A 'picture' of the sound produced by one aircraft is shown below.

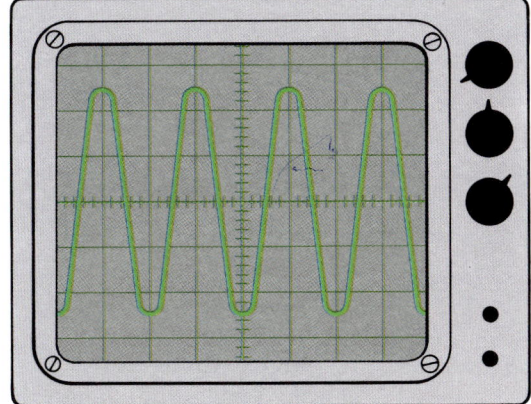

a What did the students have to connect to the oscilloscope to pick up the sound?

b Sketch the 'picture' they obtained when the noise became louder.

c What part of the wave increased when the sound became louder?

d If the oscilloscope shows the number of waves produced by the aircraft in 1/1000th of a second, what is the frequency of the wave?

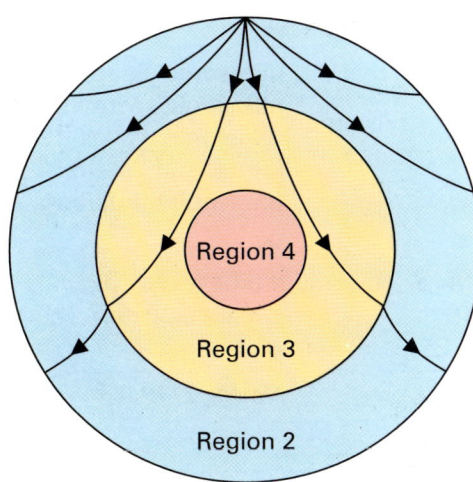

a Name each region of the Earth. Which is missing?

b What is the bending of a wave called? Why does the P wave bend?

c State two differences between a P wave and an S wave.

d Which part of the Earth is a liquid?

 Here is part of the electromagnetic spectrum.

a Copy it and fill in the two missing parts.

b Which part (i) has the lowest frequency, (ii) transfers the greatest amount of energy, (iii) causes a suntan, (iv) is given out by radioactive materials, (v) is used in communication, (vi) is absorbed by our skin and felt as heat, and (vii) is the retina sensitive to?

radio-waves		infra-red	visible	ultra-violet	gamma	

 Look at the following information about different models of the atom.

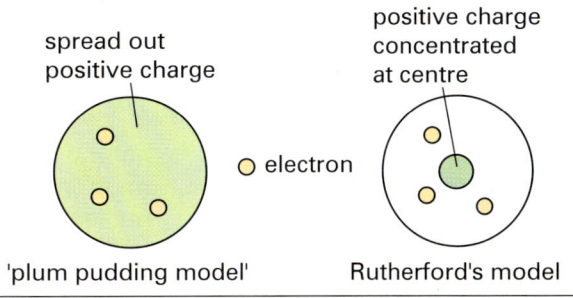

a Look at the 'plum pudding' model of the atom. What do the plum and the main part of the pudding in this model represent?

b How does the Rutherford model differ from the plum pudding model?

The diagram below shows you what you would expect to happen when positive alpha particles are used as high speed 'bullets' and fired at a positive charge.

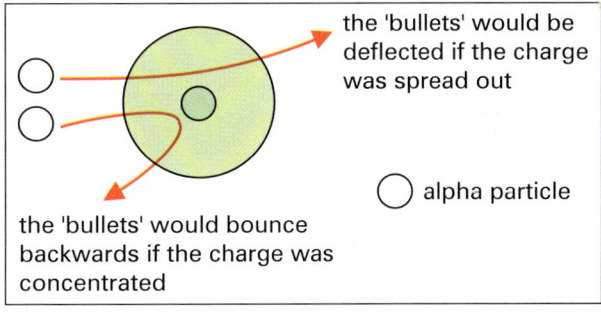

c Rutherford found that when he fired alpha particles at an atom some of them bounced backwards. Explain why this result fits his model of the atom rather than the 'plum pudding' model.

Index